Founders

FAMOUS FRIENDS

by
Jeri A. Carroll
and
Candace B. Wells

illustrated by Tom Foster

Cover by Tom Foster

Copyright © Good Apple, Inc., 1986

ISBN No. 0-86653-345-1

Printing No. 987654321

GOOD APPLE, INC.
BOX 299
CARTHAGE, IL 62321

The purchase of this book entitles the buyer to reproduce student activity pages for classroom use only. Any other use requires written permission from Good Apple, Inc.

All rights reserved. Printed in the United States of America.

We hope that Michael, Callie, and Molly are but three of the children under the age of 5 who will profit from and enjoy the stories and activities in *Founders*.

Jeri Carroll is in Early Childhood Education at Wichita State University.

Candace Wells is in Social Studies Education at Wichita State University.

Tom Foster is on faculty at Western Kentucky University.

Founders

TABLE OF CONTENTS

Introduction v
    Time Lines vii
    Kids' Books viii

Miles Standish, John Alden, & Priscilla Mullens 1
    QUESTIONS AND ACTIVITIES 7
    WORK SHEET 8

Pocahontas and John Smith 9
    QUESTIONS AND ACTIVITIES 15
    WORK SHEET 16

Benjamin Franklin 17
    QUESTIONS AND ACTIVITIES 23
    WORK SHEET 24

Betsy Ross 25
    QUESTIONS AND ACTIVITIES 31
    WORK SHEET 32

Paul Revere 33
    QUESTIONS AND ACTIVITIES 39
    WORK SHEET 40

Sacajawea 41
    QUESTIONS AND ACTIVITIES 47
    WORK SHEET 48

Daniel Boone 49
    QUESTIONS AND ACTIVITIES 55
    WORK SHEET 56

INTRODUCTION

Working with young children and history is not at all difficult. Certainly one would never assume that young children could sit and recite critical facts—that Benjamin Franklin was born in 1706 in Boston, invented eyeglasses, signed the Declaration of Independence, discovered electricity, etc. However, when all this is woven into an historical story, children will listen with amazement and remember many things that become more meaningful with time and growth.

HISTORY CAN BECOME REAL TO YOUNG CHILDREN

As we talk with the children about the various historical facts and fun happenings, we need to realize that children learn about the past before they learn about the future. It's much easier to say to a young child something happened yesterday than it is to say that it will happen tomorrow. Since it has happened to them, they understand.

As we look at goals that are typically set for young children in social studies, we find ones that start with self, expand through family, friends, schools, communities, cities, states, countries, etc. However, a closer examination of the curricula would suggest that we also present materials on human dignity, respect for human life, an appreciation for the rights of others, survival, interdependence, economy, making choices, ethnicity, relating to others, and the uniqueness of individuals.

Founders is a book designed to present the young children with important information about the people who founded this nation. The order of presentation in this book is chronological. We have tried to represent various races and sexes and hope the children will see that everyone can be an important person.

IN THIS BOOK YOU WILL FIND:

A factual story about a famous person that can be read to kids.

A suggested time of the year in which the person can be presented to tie in with other parts of the curriculum.

A suggested time line for use in the classroom.

A list of follow-up activities.

Vocabulary and discussion questions for use with each story.

Additional facts to present to the children as they are ready.

Markers or symbols for a map to be placed in your room to show children where things happened in relation to where they are.

A list of additional resources.

Work sheets to reproduce for the children.

TIME LINES

It is hoped that one of your walls is long—long enough to put up a time line. This "line" for young children cannot be a line as you might picture it.

It must be one onto which things can be drawn, placed, etc., to show the various things that are happening.

We are suggesting that a section on the time line be set off for the 1900s, one for the 1800s, one for the 1700s, and one for before and after those times. As we present the stories, we have used the terms

many, many years ago to indicate the 1700s and before,
many years ago for the 1800s,
years ago for the early 1900s, and
more recently for those things that have happened more recently in this century.

If your children have learned to read, it would be a good idea to label your sections on the time line with those italicized words.

The time line will have to be about 2' tall and the length of the room. Many things that happen during the year may be placed on the time line. For example:
1. Take a picture of your class and place it at the present.
2. Have the children bring pictures of themselves when they were babies, and place these on the time line at the year they were born.

3. Have the children bring pictures of their parents and place these where appropriate.
4. Children may have photos at home of historical events. You can place these on the appropriate dates.
5. Before you start this series of stories, brainstorm with the children and ask them what they know about what happened a long time ago. Place some of these events on the time line. See if they can project what might happen years from now. Put these events off the end of the time line.

KIDS' BOOKS

Included in this book are pages that may be cut out or duplicated to make a book to read to the kids. All you need to do is fold the three pages together. If you have access to a copy machine and wish to make a booklet for each child, simply run the desired number of copies through the machine. Then turn over both the original and the copies and run through the machine again.

On the back of each book are the new vocabulary words and a list of other resources.

SUGGESTIONS FOR USING THE KIDS' BOOKS

Color the illustrations.

Make one book for you to read to the children, or make four books and tape the story to have at a listening center with earphones.

Make enough copies for the entire class to use and take home to share with their parents.

Use the books as supplemental reading.

SUGGESTIONS FOR USING THE WORK SHEETS

Each work sheet has a picture of the FAMOUS FRIEND at the top and six squares at the bottom. Each square is a cue to an interesting fact about the life of the FAMOUS FRIEND. The work sheets can be used in many ways. The following suggestions are in order of difficulty with easier things for younger children first.

Color the pictures on the page. Put them all in a folder, and take them home to share with parents. Make covers for them.

Color and cut out all the squares at the bottoms of the pages and laminate. Use the cards for games. Each child chooses one and guesses who fits the cue.

Cut out the pictures and put them in order of presentation in the story.

Color, cut out and paste the square on a 3" x 6" piece of paper. Write the one-word cue on the right side.

Color, cut out and paste the square in the corner of a 6" x 9" piece of paper. Write an explanation of how the cue relates to the FAMOUS FRIEND.

Miles Standish, John Alden, & Priscilla Mullens

Miles Standish was born in 1584 and died in 1656. He was seventy-two years old when he died. He is best known for being a member of the governing council of Plymouth for twenty-nine years when America was still a group of English colonies.

John Alden was born in 1599 and died in 1687. He was eighty-eight years old when he died. He is best known for founding one of the colonies, Duxbury, with Miles Standish in 1641.

Vocabulary

Pilgrim
invented
bachelors
legend

Resources

The Courtship of Miles Standish, Longfellow.
If You Sailed on the Mayflower, McGovern.
If You Lived in Colonial Times, McGovern.
John Alden, Burt (Early Childhood Series).
Miles Standish, Stevenson (Early Childhood Series).

Notes for Adults

Miles Standish, John Alden and Priscilla Mullens are Pilgrims and can be added to the stories presented to children at Thanksgiving time to show that the Pilgrims were real people with names, skills, duties, and human feelings.

These three people are also associated with others at about this time in history: Pocahontas and John Smith. Compare the stories of each of these.

The children are learning to recognize a threesome, two men and one woman, as the symbol for Miles, John, and Priscilla.

John Alden was very surprised. Priscilla was in love with him and not Miles Standish. John Alden was also unhappy. He felt that he could no longer be friends with Miles Standish. John and Priscilla went together to Miles to tell him that they loved each other. As a good friend would, Miles understood. Miles watched on the happy day when John Alden and Priscilla were married.

Many, many years ago a group of people called Pilgrims set up a town in the area of the United States now called Massachusetts. *Pilgrim* is a name for a person who has travelled many, many miles. The people who settled in Massachusetts had indeed travelled many, many miles. They had sailed to this country on a ship from England.

Priscilla listened carefully to the words that John Alden spoke for Miles Standish. John told Priscilla of Miles' deep love for her and why he would be a good husband. When John had finished speaking, Priscilla looked at him and said, "Speak for yourself, John Alden."

When the Pilgrims were in England, they were treated badly by their neighbors. Their neighbors did not like the Pilgrims because they did not worship God in the same way that the neighbors did. The Pilgrims decided to find a place where they could worship God as they wanted. They decided to sail to Massachusetts.

Miles knew that his friend John Alden wrote and spoke well. After all, John kept the record of the town. Miles asked his friend, John, to speak to Priscilla for him. John agreed because Miles Standish was his friend.

It would have been convenient for the Pilgrims to fly to Massachusetts in an airplane. Unfortunately for the Pilgrims, the airplane had not yet been *invented*. The Pilgrims had to sail in a ship, and it was called the *Mayflower*. It landed in Massachusetts at a place called Plymouth. This is where the Pilgrims set up their town.

Miles Standish fell in love with Priscilla. He secretly hoped that she loved him, also. Miles wanted to tell Priscilla about his love for her, but he could not because he was trained only as a soldier. Miles had not been trained to speak and write beautiful words.

Miles Standish, John Alden, and Priscilla Mullens were all Pilgrims. They all lived in the town of Plymouth. Miles Standish was called Captain because he carried a gun to protect the town. John Alden, his friend, was the man assigned to keep a written record of what happened in the community. Both men shared a home because they were *bachelors*.

Priscilla we know about only through *legend*. That is to say, we cannot prove that Priscilla ever lived, but people talk about her as if she did. According to legend, Priscilla was the loveliest woman in the town. She was not married.

Questions and Activities

MILES STANDISH, JOHN ALDEN, & PRISCILLA MULLENS

Discussion Questions

1. Can you remember other stories about people who lived in the time when these three people lived? What things are similar about the others and these people?

2. Did you ever want to tell someone something and were embarrassed to do so? How did you feel? How did you finally solve the problem?

3. What do you think Miles learned when he was trained to be a soldier?

4. What do you think John learned when he was trained as a writer?

5. Have you ever written letters to someone? Who did the writing for you? Why did you have them do the writing?

Activities

1. Let the children draw pictures of what they think these people might have looked like in their Pilgrim outfits. (Get a copy of Ann McGovern's book, *If You Lived in Colonial Times,* and read to them the description.)

2. Draw a large ship as the *Mayflower* and have the children draw their own faces with male or female Pilgrim hats on. Cut the faces out and place above the ship, looking out over the railing. Use this on the bulletin board at Thanksgiving.

3. Place the symbol for these people on the time line at the appropriate place and on a map of the United States.

4. Get a globe or map and have the children trace the path that the *Mayflower* might have followed. They will learn that these people did not just appear here, but had to come from another land.

5. Prepare a meal that colonists might have eaten. Tell the children that the children of colonial times ate with no utensils and were not allowed to talk during the meal. They also had to stand to eat. Have the children try it for part of the meal and eat the other part as we would. Compare the two and see which they like the best.

6. Have the children draw pictures of a lamp, car, outfit of clothing. After reading this story, ask them what might have been used in the "olden" times for these things and draw those things opposite the lamp, car, and clothing.

Pocahontas and John Smith

Pocahontas was born in 1595 and died in 1617. She was only twenty-two years old when she died. She was born in what is now Virginia. She was best known for getting the release of Captain John Smith from the Indian tribe where her father was chief.

John Smith was born in 1580 and died in 1631. He was fifty-one years old when he died. He was born in England, which is in Europe. He is best known for founding the Jamestown colony in the country of America, May 24, 1607.

Vocabulary

eastern seaboard
exploring
explorer

Resources

John Smith, Barton (Childhood of Famous Americans Series).

Pocahontas, Seymour (Childhood of Famous Americans Series).

If You Lived in Colonial Times, McGovern.

Notes to Adults

The traditional time to study Indians is in November with the celebration of the first Thanksgiving feast. Pocahontas was one of the Indians who helped the colonists and encouraged the Indians to get along with the "white man."

Pocahontas and John Smith can be studied together to show that people try to get along with one another and help one another at any time of the year as you study about helping behaviors.

The children are learning to recognize the face of an Indian woman and the face of a colonist as the symbols for Pocahontas and John Smith.

Captain John Smith continued to lead the Englishmen who lived in Jamestown. He also continued to explore the lands of the New World and wrote many books about his adventures. Many people read these books so that they could learn about the New World. Captain Smith and Pocahontas had shown that very different people could get along as friends.

Many, many years ago, two children were born who would become famous Americans. One, a boy, was born in the country of England. His name was John Smith.

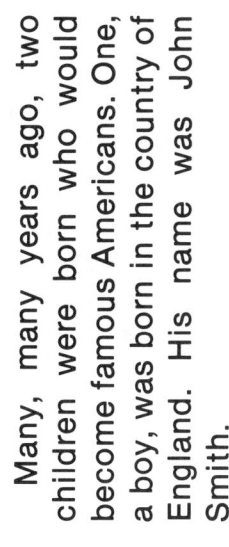

The other was a girl, an Indian princess who was born in the territory along the *eastern seaboard* of the New World (what is now the United States). This Indian princess was called Pocahontas.

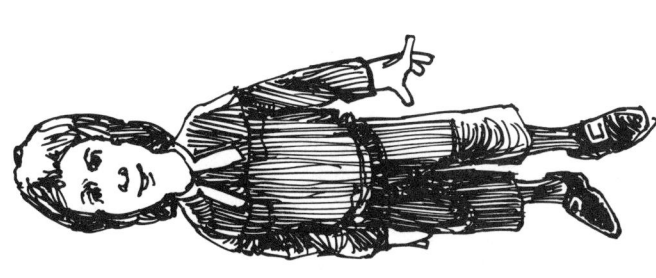

Pocahontas became friends with many of the Englishmen who lived in Jamestown. She met a young man named John Rolfe and fell in love. She and John were married and travelled to England so that Pocahontas could get to know what England was like. The people in England also wanted to get to know her. Pocahontas died while she was in England and never returned to the New World.

John Smith was the older of the two children. As a young boy, he was very interested in *exploring* new places. At first these places were very close to his home. But as John grew older, he began to explore places that were farther and farther from his home. John became famous as an *explorer*.

Pocahontas begged her father to release Captain Smith. She argued that the Englishmen and the Indians should try even harder to be friends. Pocahontas' father listened to his daughter and released Captain Smith. He also told his tribe to try to get along with the Englishmen.

While John was busy exploring, the Indian princess named Pocahontas was growing up with her tribe called the Algonquin. Pocahontas was called a princess because her father, Powhatan, was the chief of the tribe. As chief of the tribe, he was the leader of all people. He taught Pocahontas to be a leader, also.

The Englishmen and the Indian tribe did not know much about each other. They didn't even speak the same language. They tried to be friends, but it is sometimes hard to be friends when you do not know each other and do not speak the same language. One day Captain John Smith and a group of the Indians had a quarrel. The Indians took Captain Smith as their prisoner.

After John Smith had explored all of the lands that were close to England, he decided to explore the lands called the New World. The New World was where Pocahontas and her tribe lived. These lands were called the New World because the people in England had only recently become aware of them.

John Smith led a group of Englishmen to explore the New World. As their leader, John was given the title of Captain. John and his group of Englishmen founded a small town called Jamestown in the same area in which Pocahontas and her tribe lived.

Questions and Activities

POCAHONTAS AND JOHN SMITH

Discussion Questions

1. Have you ever been to the East Coast? That is where these two people lived. Let's find it on a map and on a globe. What can you tell me about the place that they lived?

2. How do you think John felt when he was captured by the Indians? Why do you think they captured him?

3. Why do you think Pocahontas wanted to have John saved?

4. Have you ever explored in a wooded area? That is what John had to do. He didn't know what was there. How do you think he felt as an explorer? How did you feel when you explored your woods or forest?

5. How do you suppose the Indians and the settlers could tell one another what they wanted if they couldn't talk with each other?

Activities

1. Place the symbol for Pocahontas and John Smith on the time line and on the map.

2. Use Lincoln Logs and let the children build a settlement. Use cones of paper for the children to decorate as teepees, and place them a distance from the settlement. The children can come up with a way to devise a forest in between. Using plastic play people, let the children reenact the story, and remind them that when they meet each other they cannot talk with each other. They have to find other ways to communicate.

3. Use large plain grocery sacks to make buckskin clothes for the children. The edges can be frayed and the brown paper painted with Indian designs (beadwork). Be sure that you do not stereotype the Indians with headbands, feathers, and war paint. That is confusing several issues. Have the children choose to be settlers or Indians, and let them act out the story of John Smith and Pocahontas.

4. Have the children draw pictures to tell the story. Show them that their pictures tell a story just as sign language did for the Indians.

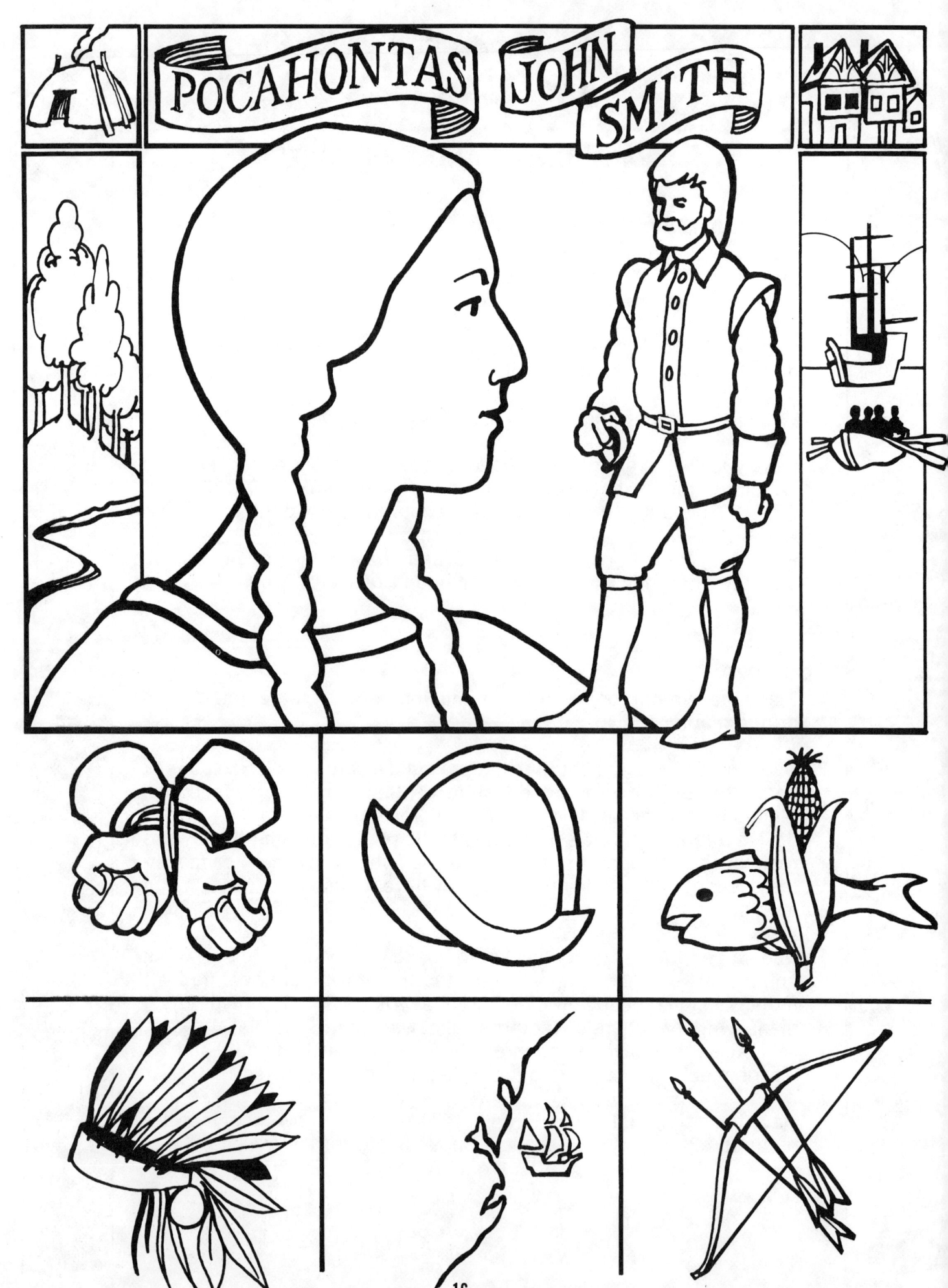

Benjamin Franklin

Benjamin was born in 1706 and died in 1790. He was eighty-four when he died. He was born in Boston, Massachusetts. He is noted for the fact that he signed the Declaration of Independence and the Constitution and started public hospitals and libraries.

Vocabulary

inventor
electricity
author
proverbs
patriot
diplomat

Resources

A Book About Benjamin Franklin, Gross.
What's the Big Idea, Ben Franklin, Fritz.
Ben Franklin of Old Philadelphia, Cousins.
Benjamin Franklin, d'Aulaire.

It is hard for an empty sack to stand upright

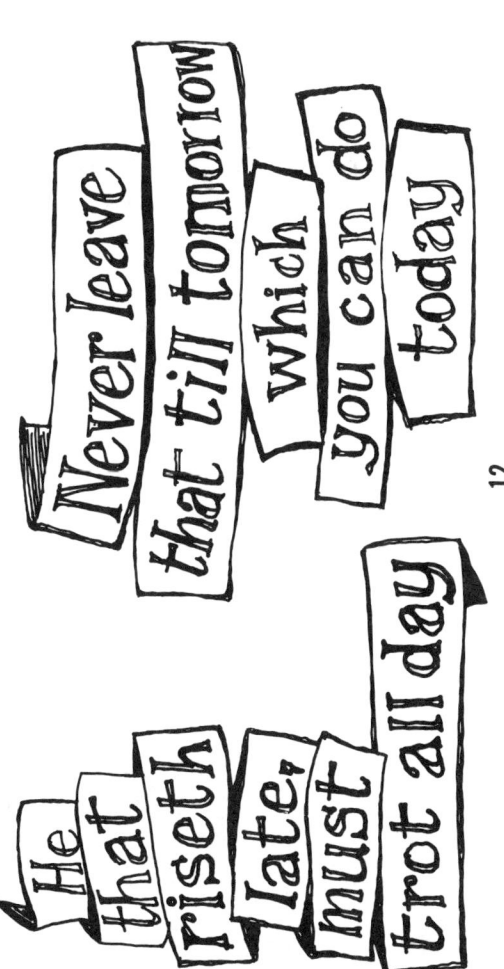

Never leave that till tomorrow which you can do today

He that riseth late, must trot all day

Notes to Adults

If you can be spontaneous, one of the best times to talk about Benjamin Franklin is during a thunderstorm. If you would like to plan the story for some other time during the year, you might do it before you go to the library. Can you imagine if we didn't have libraries?

Benjamin also had much to do with the founding of our country. There are three people in this book dealing specifically with the founding of our country: Benjamin Franklin, Paul Revere, and Betsy Ross.

The children are learning to recognize a kite and a key as the symbol for Benjamin Franklin.

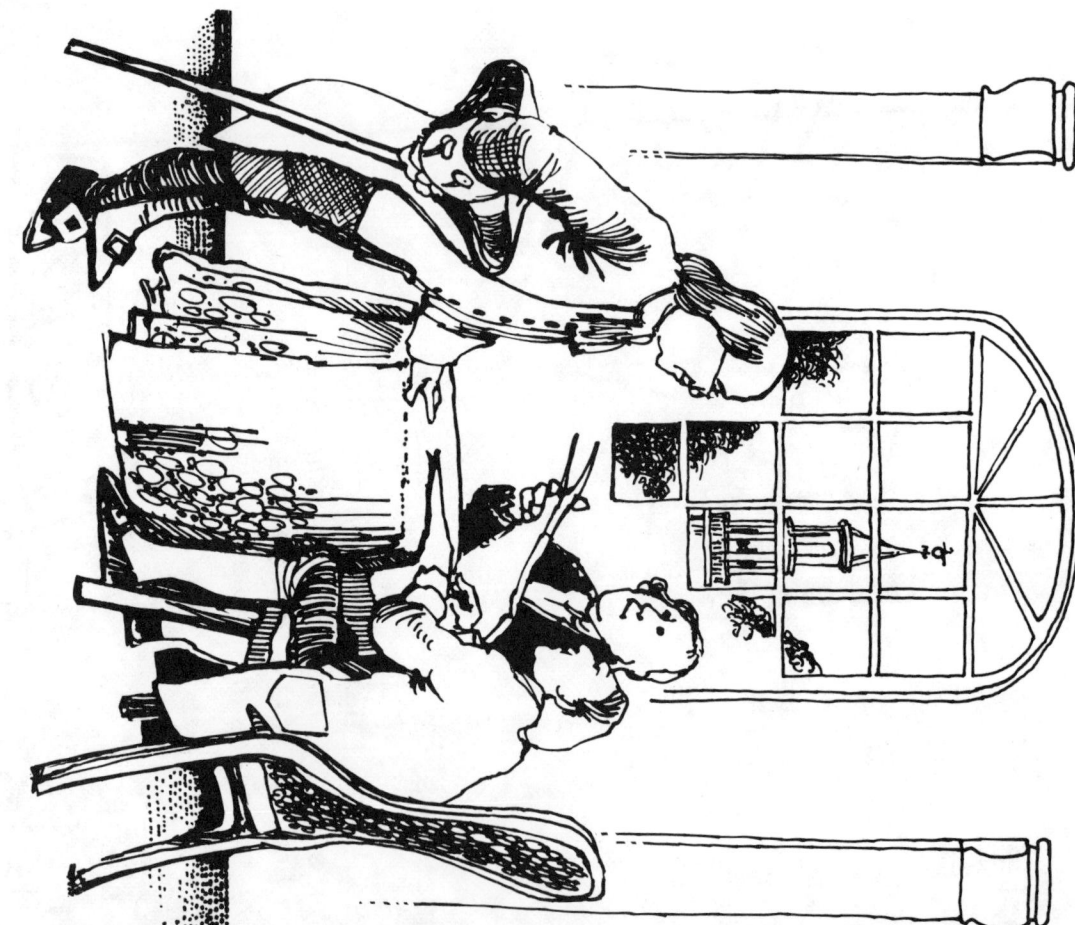

Today we think of Benjamin Franklin in many ways. He invented many things that help us in our everyday life. He was the author of many wise sayings which we repeat. Most importantly, he helped our country when it was young, just the way your parents help you.

Benjamin Franklin was born in the city of Boston, Massachusetts, many, many years ago. His mother and father had twelve children. Benjamin was the youngest child in the family. The family was poor but happy. Because the family was so poor, Benjamin left school when he was ten and went to work with his uncle, who was a printer.

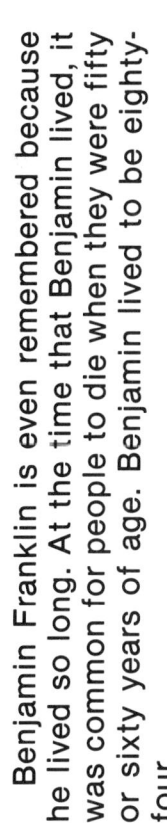

Benjamin Franklin is even remembered because he lived so long. At the time that Benjamin lived, it was common for people to die when they were fifty or sixty years of age. Benjamin lived to be eighty-four.

Benjamin was not happy staying in Boston and being a printer with his uncle, though. He wanted to know what other cities were like. He packed his few belongings and left Boston to finally settle in Philadelphia. Within a few years, he had married a young woman named Debbie. They later had one son, William.

When Benjamin went to live in another country, Debbie, his wife, and William went also. Debbie would make a comfortable home for the family, while William would help his father with his work as a diplomat. After many years of living in other countries, Debbie decided to stay home while Benjamin and William went to England. Debbie died while Benjamin and William were gone, and they returned home very sad.

As a young man, Benjamin spent a great deal of time wondering about what he could make that would help other people. Benjamin was an *inventor*. He knew that fireplaces did not keep homes warm enough, and so he invented a stove to keep homes comfortable. Benjamin made eyeglasses to help people see better. Before Benjamin made glasses, people with poor vision just had to see things blurry. Benjamin set up the first post office so that people could mail letters to each other.

Although Benjamin did many things during his lifetime, he is best remembered as a *patriot*. When our country was new, even before it was called the United States, Benjamin wrote down some ideas about how each person in a country should work together to make the country a good place to live. He also went to other countries to live and to share his ideas. When he was in another country, he was called a *diplomat*.

One day while Benjamin was wandering and flying a kite, it began to thunder and lightning. Benjamin thought about how these parts of nature could be put to good use. By tying a key to the string of a kite, Benjamin was able to show that the lightning and *electricity* were the same things.

Benjamin was also an *author*. He wrote a book for farmers that told them when to plant their seeds. To make the book funny, Benjamin thought of *proverbs* to include. Many of these sayings became famous when the farmers repeated them again and again.

These are some of Benjamin's famous sayings:

Speak Little; Do Much

He that goes a borrowing goes a sorrowing

A SMALL LEAK WILL SINK A GREAT SHIP

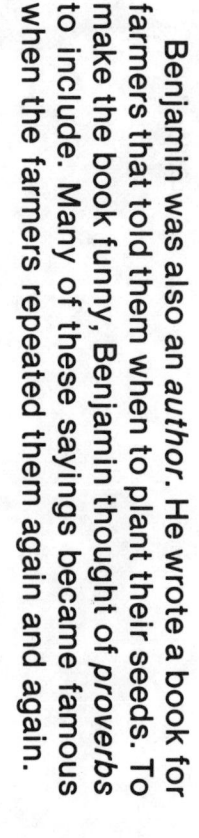

Questions and Activities

BENJAMIN FRANKLIN

Discussion Questions

1. Can you think of ways to help other people?

2. What did Benjamin Franklin do to help other people?

3. Benjamin was an inventor. He liked to think of things other people had not made before. Can you think of something that you'd like to make that hasn't been made?

4. What things did Benjamin invent?

5. What if he hadn't invented these things? What would happen if we had no post office, no mailmen, no mailboxes, no mail trucks?

6. What if we had no hospitals?

7. How do we use electricity?

8. What if we had no electricity?

Activities

1. Put Benjamin's marker on the time line to show when he lived.

2. Put Benjamin's marker on the map to show where he was born.

3. Send notes to one another and others in your school or center. Every time a note is ready, let a child hand deliver it to the next room or to the person.

4. Set up a post office. You can use boxes with dividers in them to look like post office boxes. Have a mail drop box, and let the kids sort the mail. Others may pick it up during the day. You might do this around Valentine's Day.

5. Discuss the efficiency of using a postal system.

6. Use the housekeeping area as a hospital. Get out white shirts, cotton balls, old diapers (slings), a doctor's kit, white hats, white shoes, green hospital drabs, shoes, and heat covers. Read one of the children's books about a trip to the hospital, and set the stage for the hospital center (*Curious George Goes to the Hospital*).

7. Take a trip to the library. Discuss what it would be like if there were no libraries. Let the children check books out and have them be responsible to return them. Make sure that they are involved in the whole process.

Betsy Ross

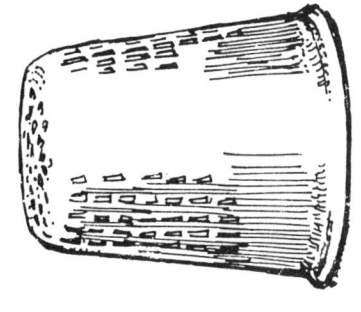

Betsy was born in 1752 and died in 1836. She was eight-four when she died.

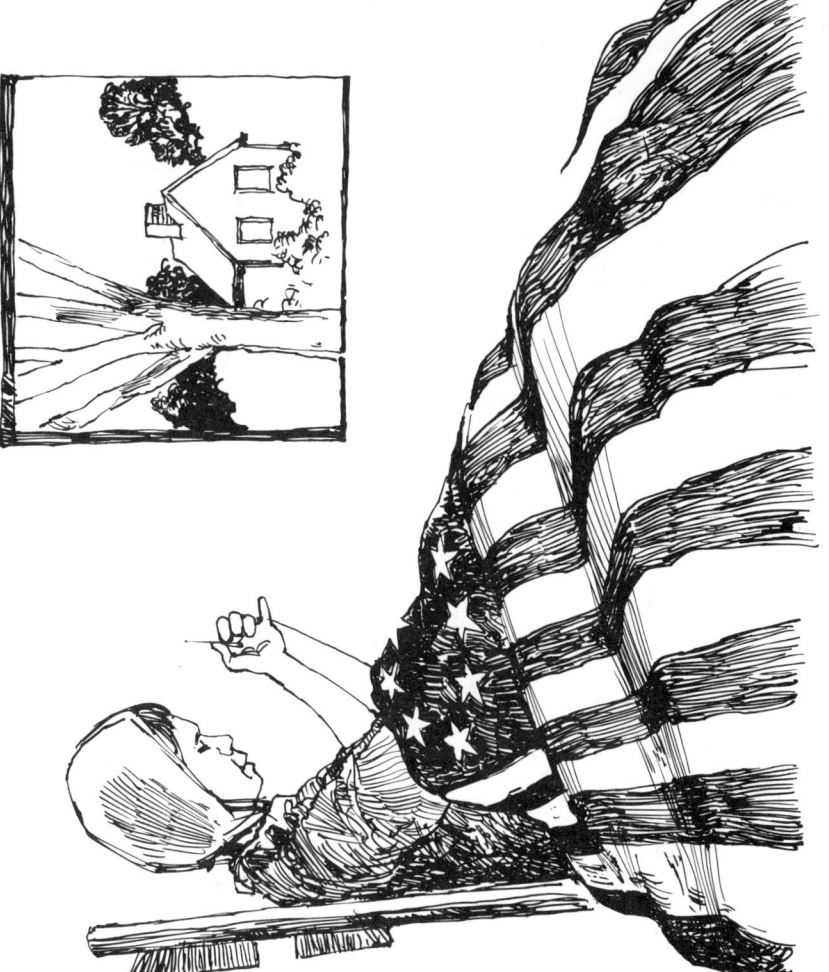

Betsy was born in Philadelphia. She is best known for the making of the first flag for the United States of America.

1

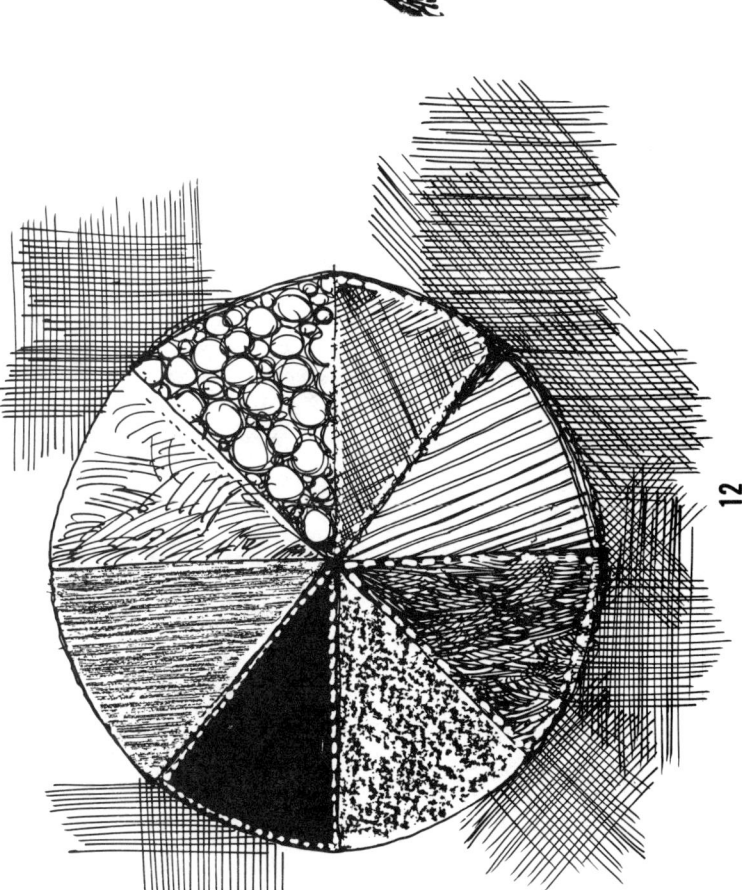

12

Vocabulary

carpenter
thimble
patchwork quilts
judged
flag

Resources

Betsy Ross, Weil (Childhood of Famous Americans Series).

If You Lived in Colonial Times, McGovern.

25

Notes to Adults

There are three times of the year that are good to talk about Betsy Ross. One is at the beginning of the year when young children are just learning about the flag. Another is Independence Day in the summer. Finally, Flag Day is June 14.

There are three people in this book dealing specifically with the founding of our country: Paul Revere, Betsy Ross, and Benjamin Franklin.

Children are learning to recognize the symbol of a woman sewing on a flag as Betsy Ross.

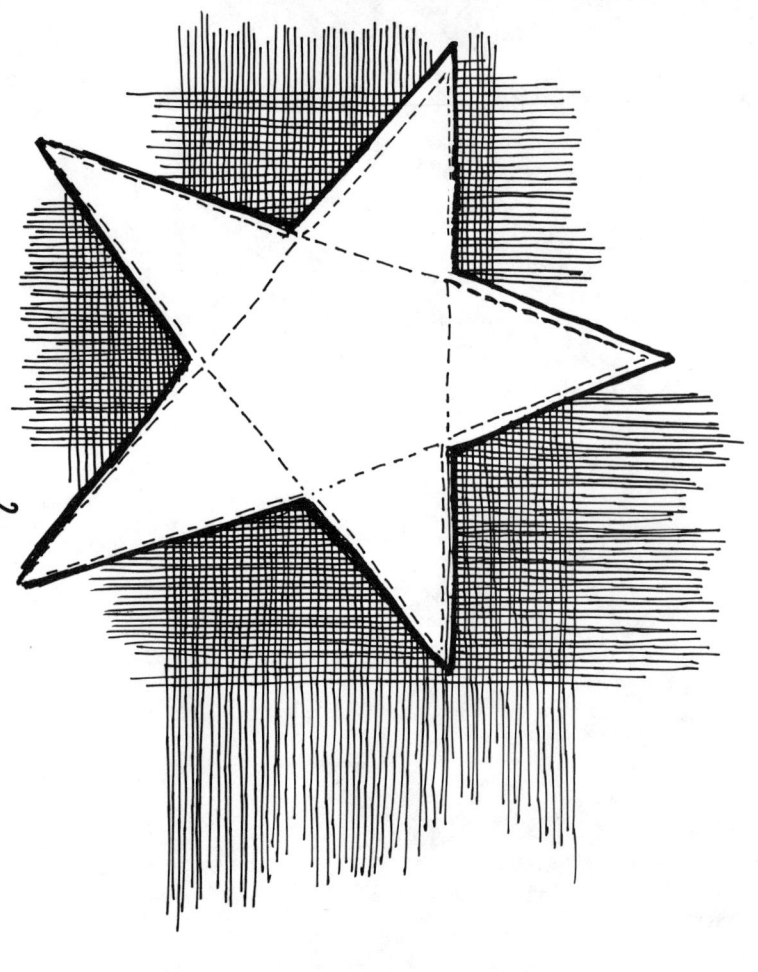

People always remember Betsy Ross when they look at the flag of the United States.

A little girl was born many, many years ago in the city of Philadelphia. Her parents named her Betsy. She had a younger brother named George. She had eight sisters. The entire family lived behind Betsy's father's workshop. He was a *carpenter*. Carpenters are people who make things out of wood.

Betsy Ross sewed many things during her lifetime. The most important thing was a flag. When the United States was just beginning, the leaders decided we needed a *flag*. They knew that Betsy Ross was the best person to sew one for them. They asked her to sew pieces of red and white stripes together for a flag. She added a patch of blue with white stars.

As a young girl, Betsy learned to sew. Her mother gave her a *thimble*, a needle, and thread. Betsy sewed small scraps of material together to make larger pieces.

When the judges had looked at the sewing, Betsy won first prize. Betsy Ross was the best sewer in the area.

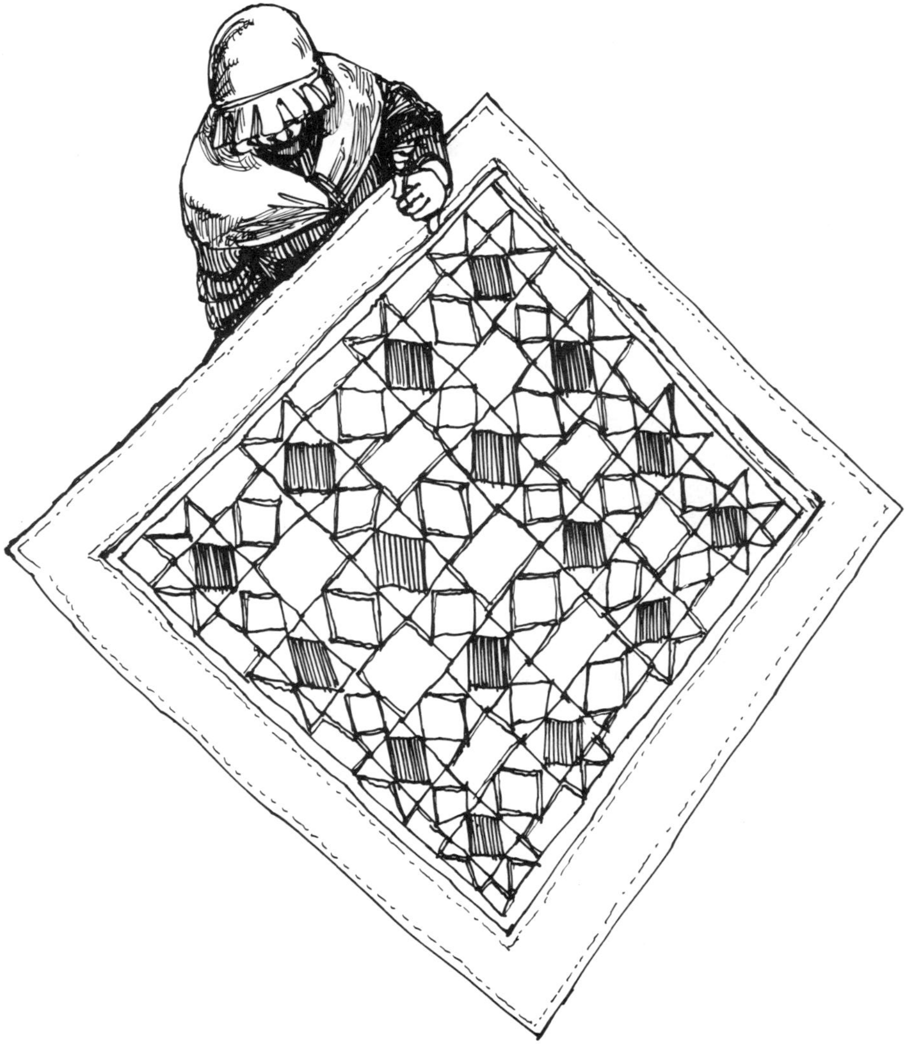

These pieces were sewn together to make even larger pieces. The larger pieces were used as blankets on the beds. These blankets were given the name of *patchwork quilts*.

The second exciting thing was a sewing contest. Betsy entered a piece of her sewing in a contest to be *judged*. There were many other women who also entered pieces of sewing. Betsy was sure that she would not win a prize. She was sure that her sewing was not as good as the others.

Betsy was very good at sewing. Her patchwork quilts were very beautiful. They were made with small, even stitches. The colors that Betsy selected for the cloth made pretty patterns. Her neighbors asked her to sew for them, also.

When Betsy was a teenager, two exciting things happened. She met a young man and fell in love. The young man's name was John Ross. The two young people were married, and Betsy's name was now Betsy Ross.

Questions and Activities

BETSY ROSS

Discussion Questions

1. Do you know how to sew? What do you use to sew? What would happen if we didn't have sewing machines? How would we sew?

2. Do you know what the American flag looks like? Let's take a good look at it. Tell me all about it. (After they tell you what they see and know, tell them the things that they haven't mentioned. Be sure to talk about the stripes standing for the number of original states, the stars for the number of states today.)

3. Have you ever heard of entering your sewing in a contest? Where might that happen now? (This leads into talks about state fairs.)

Activities

1. Place the symbol on the map and time line to locate Betsy's place of birth and time of her life.

2. Bring in a patchwork quilt for the children to examine. If you cannot find one, get a piece of patched material that has not been made into a quilt. A fabric store may have some that looks patched but is not. Use that as a last resort. Let the children make patchwork designs from material scraps glued onto paper.

3. Have the children make flags by using red and white strips ½" by 9" and a blue piece 4½" by 3". They can use silver stars to lick and place on the blue. This is somewhat the same process as the making of a quilt. Be sure to show the children that our flag today is not a quilt.

4. Examine the difference between the original flag and the flag of today and talk about the differences. Also note the similarities. The flag of Betsy's time will have the stripes of the same colors and number, but the stars will vary in number—not color. If you can find pictures of how the flag changed over time, show the children those and tell them why the changes were made.

5. Have the children draw designs onto pieces of burlap—simple shapes. Using yarn and darning needles, let them stitch around their pictures.

Paul Revere

Paul was born on New Year's Day 1735 and died in 1818. He lived to be eighty-three years of age. He was born in Boston, Massachusetts. He was known for the famous ride he took to warn the people of the war that was to begin.

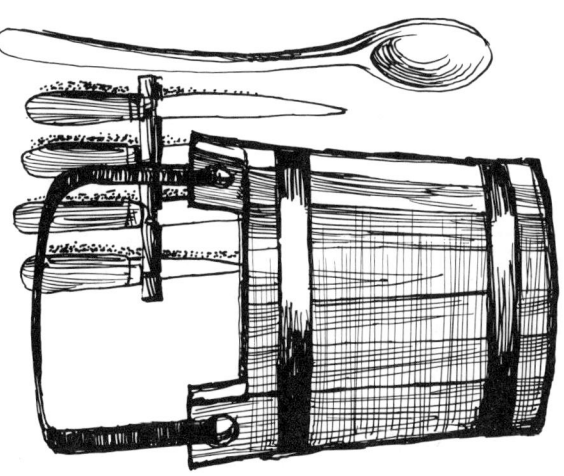

Vocabulary

silversmith
utensils
harbor
lockets
express rider
warn

Resources

And Then What Happened, Paul Revere? Fritz.
Paul Revere's Ride, a Dandelion Book.
Paul Revere, Stevenson (Childhood of Famous Americans Series).

Notes to Adults

One of the most ideal times to study about Paul Revere is in April, on or about the eighteenth as the poem indicates.

If you cannot find the time during the regular school year, try the summer when you are studying Independence Day. There are three people in this book that tell us about those who were important in the founding of our nation: Paul Revere, Betsy Ross, and Benjamin Franklin.

Children are learning to recognize Paul Revere by a rider on a horse. The rider is dressed in the costume of the 1700's.

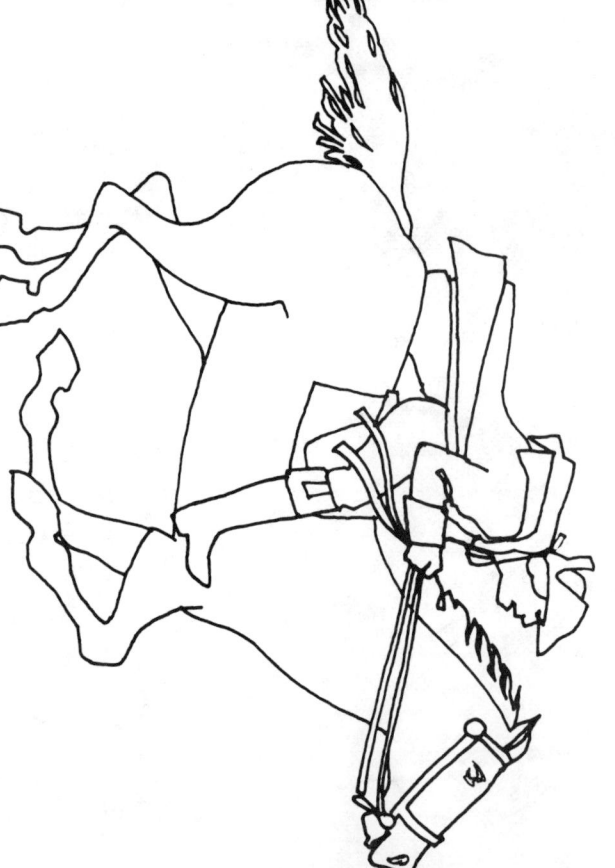

He rode all night from small town to small town to *warn* the people. When the fighting began, the people that Paul had warned were ready for the war and the United States remained free of English rule.

Paul Revere was born many, many years ago in Boston, Massachusetts. He was born on the same day that the new year started, New Year's Day. He had a mother, father, and an older sister. His father made household *utensils* of gold and silver. He was a *goldsmith* and *silversmith*.

Paul Revere became famous for an express ride that he took when a war was about to start. The United States was seeking to be free from English rule—the king of England was trying to tell us what to do instead of letting us decide for ourselves, and Paul knew that it was important for the people in the neighboring towns to know that a war was about to begin.

As a young child, Paul loved to walk the streets of Boston, which is near the ocean. It has a large *harbor* with many sailing ships which were quite beautiful when they were sailing in the harbor. There was always something interesting at the harbor for Paul to see.

The person who was riding the horse would tell the news in each town as he went. The person riding the horse was called an express rider. Paul Revere became the best express rider in the whole area.

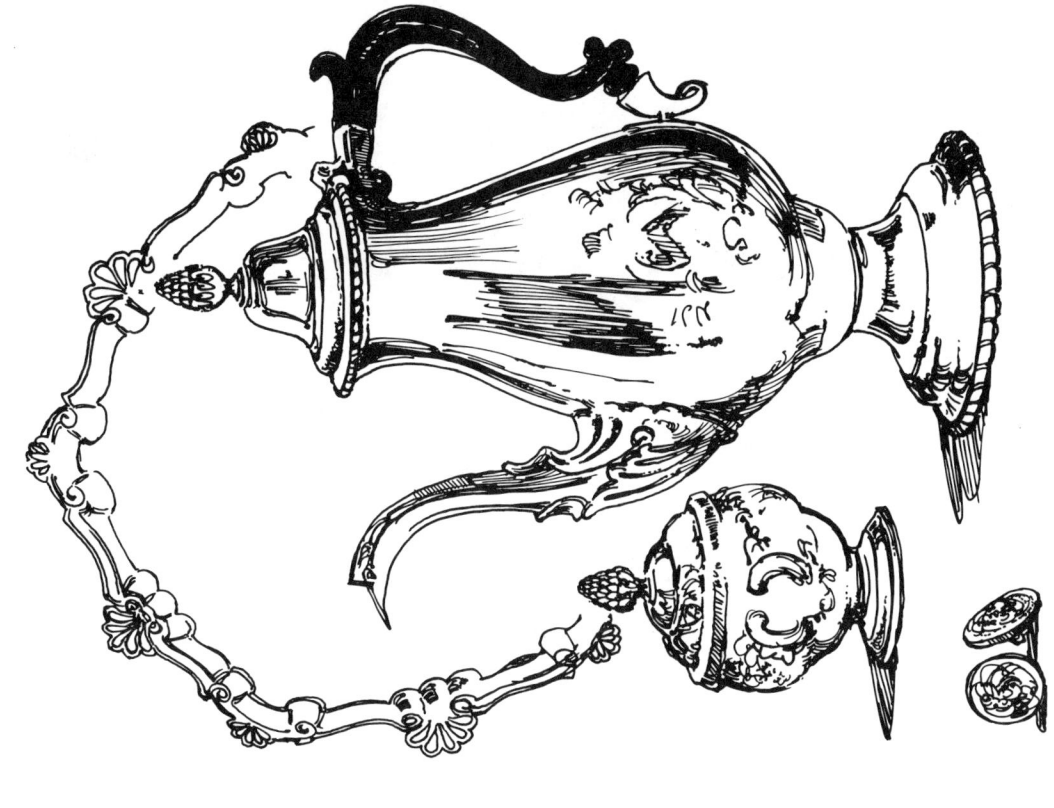

When he was fifteen years old, his father died. Paul took over the family business and became a silversmith like his father. He made all sorts of things out of silver for people to use in their homes, such as spoons, cups, and teapots. He made rings, bracelets, and *lockets*. He even made gold and silver buttons for coats and jackets.

One of the jobs that Paul had was as an *express rider*. In the days when people had no radios or telephones or televisions, it was difficult to get news from one place to another. People solved this problem by riding on a horse from one town to another.

Paul married a nice woman named Sarah, and they had six children. Paul loved Sarah and the children very much, but Sarah died when the children were very small. Paul married again. This time he married a woman named Rachel. Rachel took good care of Sarah's six children, and she and Paul had five more children of their own. That made eleven children in the Revere family.

With so many children, Paul decided that he needed more jobs. He couldn't make enough money as a silversmith to feed his large family. Paul took on some other jobs. He rang the church bells in the church steeple on Sunday mornings, he learned how to be a dentist, and did whatever other odd jobs he could to earn money.

Questions and Activities

PAUL REVERE

Discussion Questions

1. Have you ever heard of people going from one place to another to tell others about things that were going to happen? Tell us about them.

2. What things are made of gold and silver today? How do these things get made?

3. How many people are in your family? How do you think it would feel to be one of eleven children? What would eleven children do in a family?

4. Why did Paul Revere have to have so many jobs? What were those jobs?

5. Do you know any times now that a bell is used to tell us things?

Activities

1. Be sure to put the marker up on the map to mark the place where Paul Revere was born.

2. Place the marker on the time line to show when he was born.

3. Bring in things made of gold and silver, including a Revere bowl. Talk about how they are and were made.

4. Read the poem of Paul Revere—"On the eighteenth of April, in seventy-five,/Hardly a man is now alive/Who remembers that famous day and year" of the midnight ride of Paul Revere.

5. One day when it is time for school to be dismissed, send a messenger to tell the rooms instead of ringing the bell. Talk about the benefits and troubles with that.

6. Bring in a collection of different kinds of bells, and have the children examine them and ring each of them. Talk about the similarities and differences in the bells. Have the children bring in bells from home to share. After putting their names on them and listening to their bells, put them in a group behind a sheet. Sit behind the sheet and ring a bell. See if the owner can identify it by sound.

Sacajawea

Sacajawea was born in 1788 and died in 1884.
She was ninety-six years old when she died.
She was born in the area of what is now Idaho.
Sacajaewa helped lead many explorations in the western United States.
She was born a Shoshoni Indian.

Vocabulary

tribe
teepees
herbs
trapper
explored
knowledge

Resources

The Pioneers, Gorsline.
North American Indians, Gorsline.
Sacajawea, Seymour (Childhood of Famous Americans Series).

Notes to Adults

Sacajawea was an Indian woman who led people in parts they had not previously been. She can be studied at a time when we usually study Indians—at Thanksgiving—but better yet at a time when we have had a guide on a field trip who has shown us many things that are new. Many times this is at the first of the year when the children themselves are new to a school situation.

Sacajawea is one of two people in this book who were settlers. The other is Daniel Boone. Children are learning to recognize a teepee as the symbol for Sacajawea.

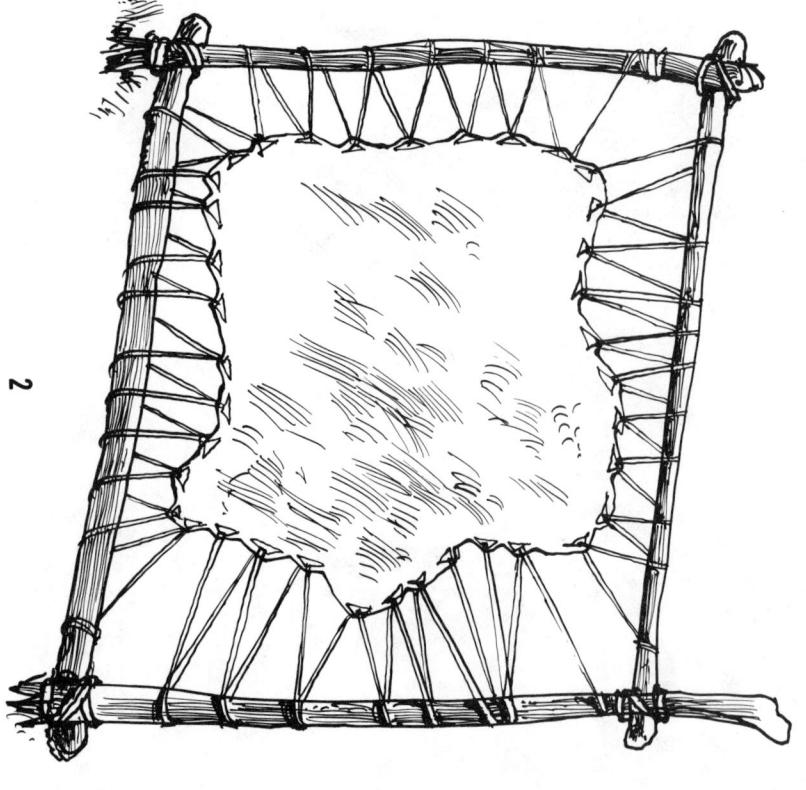

Today we are grateful to Sacajawea because she shared her *knowledge* with men who needed it. Describing the land was very important to Lewis and Clark. They could not have succeeded if Sacajawea had not helped them.

Many, many years ago a baby girl was born into a *tribe* of Indians. This tribe was known as the Shoshoni. The baby girl was named Sacajawea, or Little Bird, because she was so small. Sacajawea and her Shoshoni family lived in the mountain regions of the western part of our country.

Sacajawea was very helpful during the long time that she traveled with Lewis and Clark. She showed the men which berries and plants they could eat. She made them medicines from the herbs she had learned about as a child. When the men's shoes wore out, she helped to make new ones from the skins of animals.

As a young girl, Sacajawea played games with the other Indian children and she helped the older people in the tribe. The men of the tribe hunted animals for food. The women of the tribe cooked the meat and used the skins for shoes and *teepees*.

4

Because they had never seen the area before, Lewis and Clark did not know as much about it as Sacajawea and her husband did. Lewis and Clark asked Sacajawea to go with them as they *explored* the land.

9

Sacajawea gathered berries to eat. She also looked for plants and *herbs* from which to make medicines. She learned much about how to use the things around her.

Two other men were important in Sacajawea's life. They were Meriwether Lewis and William Clark, better known in history as Lewis and Clark. Lewis and Clark had been hired to describe the area in which Sacajawea and her husband lived and make the first maps of the area.

When Sacajawea was grown, she married a *trapper*. This man would capture animals in traps and sell them to others so that the fur of the animals could be made into coats and blankets.

Sacajawea and her husband traveled from place to place in order to find the animals.

Questions and Activities

SACAJAWEA

Discussion Questions

1. Have you ever gone someplace you've never been before? How did you feel? What was exciting about it?

2. When someone new comes to our room, we assign that person a friend for a few days to help out with questions the new student might have. Why do we do that? How is that like what Sacajawea did for Lewis and Clark?

3. How could a trapper trap animals? What types of animals could they have used for clothing?

4. What might have happened to Lewis and Clark if Sacajawea had not helped them?

Activities

1. Put Sacajawea's marker on the map to locate where she was born.

2. Put her marker on the time line to show when she lived.

3. Set up an obstacle course and show one person how to get through it. Then let that person guide the others.

4. Set up a "road through the past" by having tables in the hallways with "old" things on them. Guide the children through the past.

5. Do some basic map skills with the group. On a large floor plan of the room, let them place blocks to represent tables, chairs, etc.

6. Paint white cloth with edible berries. Let the kids both eat the berries and use them as dye. Try the ones that stain your clothes the best—blueberries as a starter.

7. Set up a treasure map for the kids to follow, and at the treasure spot have a set of Indian artifacts or the snack for the day.

8. Build a life-sized teepee in the classroom, and let the kids paint Indian signs on the sheets to cover the poles.

9. Have the children make costumes of the time with paper sacks. They look great as buckskin. As you read the story again, let the children act it out and guide the frontiersmen along the path to where they are heading.

Daniel Boone

Daniel was born in 1734 and died in 1820.
He lived to be eighty-six years old.
He was born in Reading, Pennsylvania.
He was best known as a guide in the wilderness.

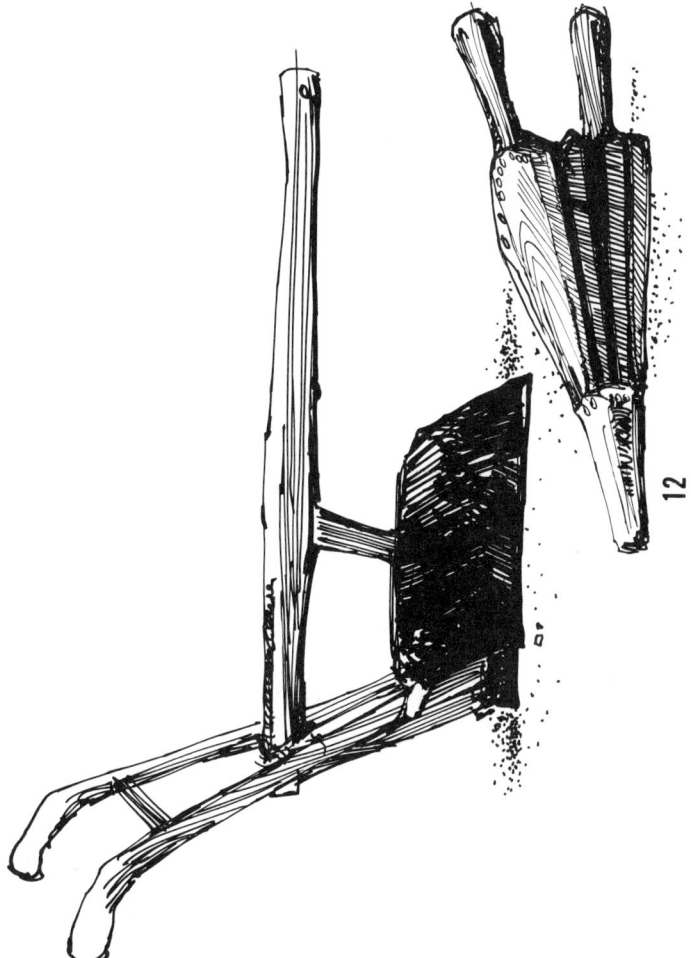

Vocabulary
blacksmith
plow
bellows
forge
wilderness
tracker
responsibilities

Resources
Daniel Boone, Frontier Adventures, Brandt.
Daniel Boone, Stevenson (Childhood of Famous Americans Series).

Notes to Adults

Daniel Boone can be studied at the first of any new adventure—a trip to school, a field trip to the zoo, a trip just about anywhere. He was an explorer going some place new. Children can understand some of the anxieties as they venture forth to new places.

There is another settler in this book: Sacajawea. She can be studied now or at another time.

Children are learning to recognize the bellows that Daniel learned to dislike as the symbol for Daniel Boone.

For many years Daniel Boone showed people the way into the wilderness. People thanked Daniel by naming towns after him. This was a way that some towns got their names. Daniel Boone was indeed a special person.

On a farm in Pennsylvania many, many years ago, a baby boy was born to Squire and Sarah Boone. They named their son Daniel. Daniel grew up in this family, and they eventually had eleven children. Daniel was the one right in the middle.

Other people wanted to move into the wilderness, also. They were not able to do all the things that Daniel was able to do. They needed his help, and he was glad to help these people. He showed them the way into the wilderness, serving as their guide. The road they traveled became known as the Wilderness Road.

Daniel Boone learned to walk before he was a year old. Some people say that he never stopped walking from that time on. He loved the out-of-doors and since they didn't have cars in those days, he did a lot of his walking outside. He would walk for hours around the family farm.

4

When Daniel was a young man, he decided that he wanted to live in the *wilderness*. Very few people lived in the wilderness. Daniel would have to live by himself, get his own food, and take care of himself. He could do it though because the Indians and his parents had taught him well.

9

He would walk with his family to church on Sunday. He walked to the swimming hole in the summer. As long as it was outdoors, Daniel would walk there.

When Daniel was not busy working, he walked in the woods that surrounded the farm. He made friends with the Indians who lived in the woods. Daniel learned many things from his friends. He learned how to follow an animal in the woods and how to hunt with a bow and arrow. He became the finest hunter and *tracker* in the woods.

Daniel's father was a *blacksmith* who made objects of iron for people to use. He made things as small as nails or as big as a *plow*. Daniel helped his father by pumping the *bellows* to keep the fire going in the *forge*. Mr. Boone used the forge to heat the iron so that he could hammer it into the shape he needed. However, this work was done indoors, and you know how Daniel loved to be outdoors.

Daniel's father asked him to help on the farm. Daniel was again happy. Even though the work on the farm was difficult, he liked it because he was working outside. He plowed the fields and planted corn, cut down trees for firewood and looked after the cows and chickens. He had a lot of *responsibilities*.

Questions and Activities

DANIEL BOONE

Discussion Questions

1. Daniel walked many places. Where do you walk? How else might we get there? How else might Daniel have gotten there?

2. Have you ever ridden on a horse? How was it? Do you think that you could get places as comfortably or as fast on a horse as in a car?

3. Daniel's father made nails. How do you suppose a nail could be made? Do we make nails today? How do we get nails when we need them?

4. Have you ever been camping? How is living outdoors different from living indoors? Daniel lived outdoors for long periods of time, not just one night. What were some dangers he might have encountered?

5. What is the name of your town? How did it get its name?

Activities

1. Place a marker on the map to show where Daniel Boone was born.

2. Place the marker on the time line to show when he was born.

3. Set up a wilderness where the children have to find something. Make marks to show them that they are on the right track. Have something at the end of the "path" for them as a reward—food might be good since a lot of Daniel's tracking would have been for food.

4. Have a bow and arrow there for the children to see—a play one would be much safer. The children could use it in a center if it was one with suction cup arrows.

5. Have the children make coonskin caps from paper. If you use brown construction paper, each student can cut a strip and a tail and staple the tail onto the strip. The strip can be wrapped around the head and stapled to fit.

6. Set up a campground for a center. Use logs, yellow and orange paper for fire, long sticks and a sheet for a tent. Use the coonskin caps and other fur clothing in the center, as well as a fur blanket. Use pails for water, plates, spoons, etc., for eating and pots for cooking.